The Iditarod
Racing Across Alaska

Represent and Solve Problems Involving Multiplication

Kathleen Salvitas

INFOMAX
MATH READERS

Rosen
Classroom™

New York

Published in 2015 by The Rosen Publishing Group, Inc.
29 East 21st Street, New York, NY 10010

Book Design: Mickey Harmon

Photo Credits: Cover, pp. 9, 13 Anchorage Daily News/Contributor/McClatchy-Tribune/Getty Images; pp. 3–24 (snow
border) Kuttelvaserova Stuchelova/Shutterstock.com; p. 5 (inset) AridOcean/Shutterstock.com; p. 5 (main) American Stock
Archive/Contributor/Archive Photos/Getty Images; p. 7 http://en.wikipedia.org/wiki/File:Balto.jpg; p. 11 Louise Cukrov/
Shutterstock.com; p. 15 Al Grillo/AP Images; p. 17 Tom Reichner/Shutterstock.com; p. 19 Matt Cooper/Shutterstock.com;
p. 21 Ermolaev Alexander/Shutterstock.com; p. 22 http://commons.wikimedia.org/wiki/File:Iditarod_finish_line.jpg.

ISBN: 978-1-4777-4709-4
6-pack ISBN: 978-1-4777-4705-6

Manufactured in the United States of America

CPSIA Compliance Information: Batch #WS15RC: For further information contact Rosen Publishing, New York, New York at 1-800-237-9932.

Contents

What Is the Iditarod?

The Iditarod is the most famous dogsled race in the world. Teams of dogs pull sleds across the snowy land of Alaska. The first team to get from Anchorage to the finish line in Nome is the winner. Mushers, or dogsled drivers, train with their teams for a long time to get ready for the Iditarod.

This race follows the Iditarod National Historical Trail. It was created to honor the importance of sled dogs in Alaskan history.

Sled dogs used to carry the mail, important supplies, and goods for trading across Alaska.

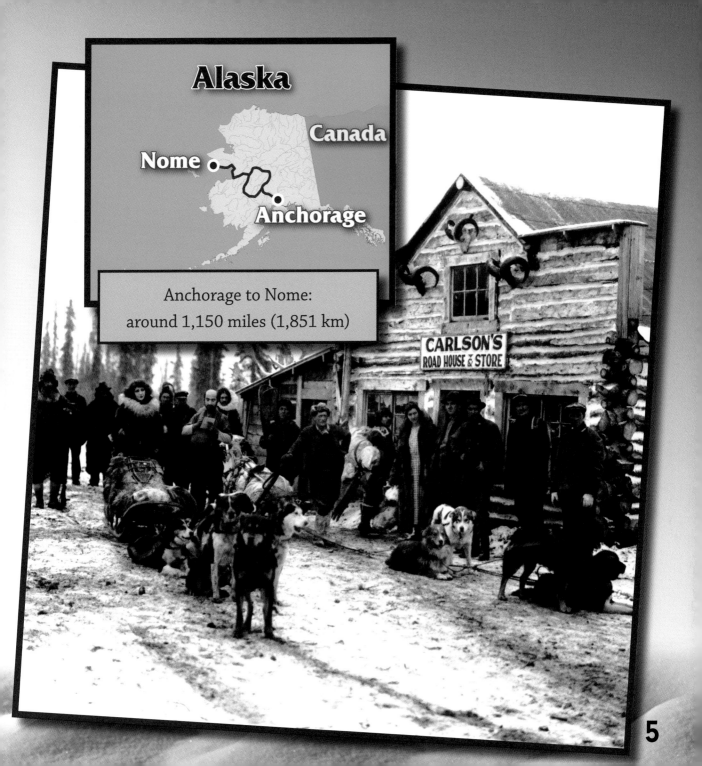

Alaska

Canada

Nome

Anchorage

Anchorage to Nome:
around 1,150 miles (1,851 km)

CARLSON'S
ROAD HOUSE & STORE

The Iditarod's History

One of the most famous dogsled runs from Anchorage to Nome took place in 1925. Children in Nome were getting sick with a deadly **disease**, and the only **medicine** for it was in Anchorage. More than 20 mushers and their sled dog teams helped get the medicine from Anchorage to Nome.

The lead sled dog of the team that finally reached Nome was named Balto. He became so famous that he toured the United States for 2 years!

> You can find out how many months Balto toured the United States by multiplying the number of years (2) by the numbers of months in 1 year (12).
> The answer is 24.

2 x 12 = 24

The Iditarod began as a much shorter race in the 1960s. It was originally created in 1967 to celebrate the 100th anniversary of Alaska becoming a U.S. territory. Then, people began working to prepare more of the Iditarod National Historical Trail for a longer race.

In 1973, the first race from Anchorage to Nome took place. The total number of mushers who finished could be split into 2 groups with 11 mushers in each group. How many mushers finished altogether?

> You can use a question mark to stand for the missing number in an equation, or math problem. In this equation, the missing number is 22.

$$2 \times 11 = \ ?$$
$$2 \times 11 = 22$$

Two Trails

The Iditarod National Historical Trail has a northern **section** and a southern section. Dogsled teams race on the northern section in even years and the southern section in odd years.

Both trails have a **series** of checkpoints. These are places where mushers can get fresh supplies and rest with their teams of sled dogs as needed. There are 27 checkpoints on the southern trail. What number, when multiplied by 3, gives you 27?

The missing number in this multiplication equation is 9. You can figure out the answer by remembering basic multiplication facts.

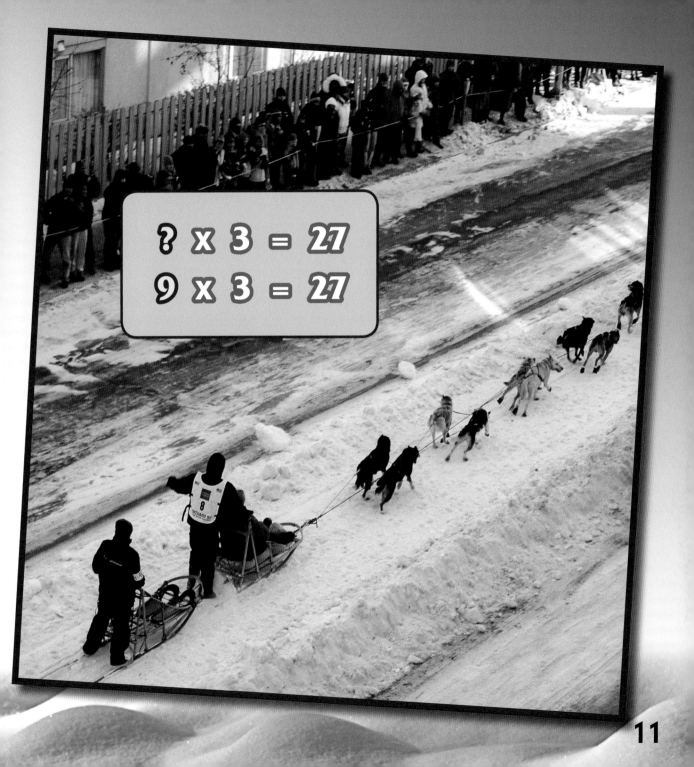

? x 3 = 27
9 x 3 = 27

The northern section of the Iditarod National Historical Trail was the section mushers first raced on. It was the only section used for years, until the southern section was opened to racers. The northern section has 26 checkpoints.

What number, when multiplied by 1, equals 26? The answer is 26. Any number multiplied by 1 equals that same number.

Sled dogs sleep in beds made of straw at checkpoints. This helps them stay warm.

Three Decades of Success

The Iditarod has many records that were set by great mushers. For example, Rick Swenson is the only musher to win the Iditarod 5 times. He won the race in 1977, 1979, 1981, 1982, and 1991. This also makes him the first musher to win the Iditarod in 3 different decades.

How many years are in 3 decades? The answer is easy to find if you know there are 10 years in 1 decade.

You can use multiplication to find the number of years in 3 decades. The answer is 30 years. That's a long time to have so much success as a musher!

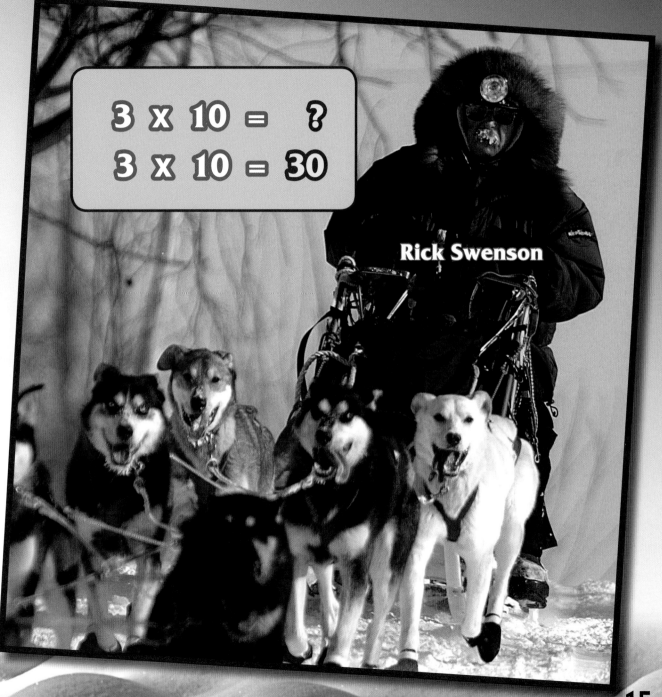

3 x 10 = ?
3 x 10 = 30

Rick Swenson

15

Many Mushers

The Iditarod has been held every year since 1973. In that time, more than 400 mushers have finished the race. These mushers have come from countries as far away as France, Norway, Italy, and even Japan!

Iditarod mushers have also come from at least 20 different U.S. states. If you were to put those 20 states into groups of 5, how many groups would there be? You can use division to find the missing number.

Division is closely related to multiplication. You can use division to find the missing number in a multiplication equation. If we know $20 \div 5 = 4$, then we also know $4 \times 5 = 20$.

$$20 \div 5 = 4$$
$$4 \times 5 = 20$$

Sled Dogs on the Trail

Over 1,000 dogs race in the Iditarod every year. The dogs work very hard pulling the sleds across the snow and ice. They wear special booties to **protect** their paws in the same way people wear boots to protect their feet from ice and snow.

Each Iditarod team has an average of 16 dogs. If those 16 dogs were divided into 2 groups, how many dogs would be in each group?

> You can set up this equation as a multiplication equation with an unknown factor. Or, you can use division to find the number that makes 16 when multiplied by 2.

$$16 = ? \times 2$$
$$16 \div 2 = ?$$

How do the people running the Iditarod keep track of so many dogs? They use special **collar** tags with combinations of letters and numbers to identify each dog. They also use microchips. These are small computer chips put safely and painlessly under a dog's skin to keep track of where it is. Each microchip has its own code with 8 **digits**.

If the dogs on a team have 96 digits from all their microchips put together, how many dogs are on that team?

How would you find the missing number
in this multiplication equation?

96 = ? x 8

An Important Tradition

When the Iditarod begins each year in Anchorage, a special lamp called the Widow's Lamp is lit at the finish line in Nome. This serves as a reminder of the lamps that were lit at roadhouses along the trail in the past. These lamps would stay lit until a team safely reached their next stop. The Widow's Lamp stays lit at the Iditarod's finish line until the last team safely finishes the race. It's a very important **tradition**!

The tradition of the Widow's Lamp connects the Iditarod's present with its past.

Glossary

collar (KAH-luhr) A band, strip, or chain worn around the neck.

digit (DIH-juht) Any of the numerals from 1 to 9 and usually the symbol 0.

disease (dih-ZEEZ) A sickness.

medicine (MEH-duh-suhn) Something people take when they are sick so they can feel better.

protect (pruh-TEHKT) To keep safe.

section (SEHK-shun) A part.

series (SIHR-eez) A number of things arranged in order and connected by being alike in some way.

tradition (truh-DIH-shun) A belief, knowledge, or way of doing things that is handed down from the past.

Index